A Christmas Treasury

VERY MERRY STORIES AND POEMS

Illustrated by

KEVIN HAWKES

HarperCollinsPublishers

To Grant

A Christmas Treasury: Very Merry Stories and Poems

Compilation and illustrations copyright © 2001 by Kevin Hawkes

Printed in the U.S.A. All rights reserved.

www.harperchildrens.com

Library of Congress Cataloging-in-Publication Data

A Christmas treasury: very merry stories and poems / illustrated by Kevin Hawkes.

p. cm.

Contents: The wind in the willows from Chapter V, Dulce Domum / Kenneth Grahame — Jolly Old Saint Nicholas / traditional carol — Christmas at the Hollow Tree Inn / Albert Bigelow Paine — The friendly beasts / traditional carol — Visit from St. Nicholas / Clement Clarke Moore.

ISBN 0-688-12039-3 (trade) — ISBN 0-688-12040-7 (lib. bdg.)

1. Christmas—Literary collections. [1. Christmas—Literary collections.] I. Hawkes, Kevin, ill.

PZ5.V45 2000   99-048761

820.8'0334—dc21

Typography by Robbin Gourley

1 2 3 4 5 6 7 8 9 10

❖

First Edition

Contents

The Wind in the Willows

KENNETH GRAHAME

A Selection from Chapter V, "Dulce Domum"

O N A C O L D D E C E M B E R N I G H T , *after many months adventuring on the open road with his friend the Water Rat, a world-weary Mole returns to his long abandoned home.*

It was close and airless, and the earthy smell was strong, and it seemed a long time to Rat ere the passage ended and he could stand erect and stretch and shake himself. The Mole struck a match, and by its light the Rat saw that they were standing in an open space, neatly swept and sanded underfoot, and directly facing them was Mole's little front door, with "Mole End" painted, in Gothic lettering, over the bell-pull at the side.

Mole reached down a lantern

from a nail on the wall and lit it, and the Rat, looking round him, saw that they were in a sort of fore-court. A garden-seat stood on one side of the door, and on the other a roller; for the Mole, who was a tidy animal when at home, could not stand having his ground kicked up by other animals into little runs that ended in earth-heaps. On the walls hung wire baskets with ferns in them, alternating with brackets carrying plaster statuary—Garibaldi, and the infant Samuel, and Queen Victoria, and other heroes of modern Italy. Down on one side of the fore-court ran a skittle-alley, with benches along it and little wooden tables marked with rings that hinted at beer-mugs. In the middle was a small round pond containing gold-fish and surrounded by a cockle-shell border. Out of the centre of the pond rose a fanciful erection clothed in more cockle-shells and topped by a large silvered glass ball that reflected everything all wrong and had a very pleasing effect.

Mole's face beamed at the sight of all these objects so dear to him, and he hurried Rat through the door, lit a lamp in the hall, and took one glance round his old home. He saw the dust lying thick on everything, saw the cheerless, deserted look of the long-neglected house, and its narrow, meagre dimensions, its worn and shabby contents—and collapsed again on a hall-chair, his nose in his paws. "O Ratty!" he cried dismally, "why ever did I do it? Why did I bring you to this poor, cold little place, on a night like this, when you might have been at River Bank by this time, toasting your toes before a blazing fire, with all your own nice things about you!"

The Rat paid no heed to his doleful self-reproaches. He was running here and there, opening doors, inspecting rooms and cupboards, and lighting lamps and candles and sticking them up everywhere. "What a capital little house this is!" he called out cheerily. "So compact! So well planned! Everything here and everything in its place! We'll make a jolly night of it. The first thing

we want is a good fire; I'll see to that—I always know where to find things. So this is the parlour? Splendid! Your own idea, those little sleeping-bunks in the wall? Capital! Now, I'll fetch the wood and the coals, and you get a duster, Mole—you'll find one in the drawer of the kitchen table—and try and smarten things up a bit. Bustle about, old chap!"

Encouraged by his inspiriting companion, the Mole roused himself and dusted and polished with energy and heartiness, while the Rat, running to and fro with armfuls of fuel, soon had a cheerful blaze roaring up the chimney. He hailed the Mole to come and warm himself; but Mole promptly had another fit of the blues, dropping down on a couch in dark despair and burying his face in his duster. "Rat," he moaned, "how about your supper, you poor, cold, hungry, weary animal? I've nothing to give you—nothing—not a crumb!"

"What a fellow you are for giving in!" said the Rat reproachfully. "Why, only just now I saw a sardine-opener on the kitchen dresser, quite distinctly; and everybody knows that means there are sardines about somewhere in the neighbourhood. Rouse yourself! pull yourself together, and come with me and forage."

They went and foraged accordingly, hunting through every cupboard and turning out every drawer. The result was not so very depressing after all, though of course it might have been better; a tin of sardines—a box of captain's biscuits, nearly full—and a German sausage encased in silver paper.

"There's a banquet for you!" observed the Rat, as he arranged the table. "I know some animals who would give their ears to be sitting down to supper with us to-night!"

"No bread!" groaned the Mole dolorously; "no butter, no—"

"No *pâté de fois gras,* no champagne!" continued the Rat, grinning. "And that reminds me—what's that little door at the end of the passage? Your cellar, of course! Every luxury in this

house! Just you wait a minute."

He made for the cellar-door, and presently reappeared, somewhat dusty, with a bottle of beer in each paw and another under each arm. "Self-indulgent beggar you seem to be, Mole," he observed. "Deny yourself nothing. This is really the jolliest little place I ever was in. Now, wherever did you pick up those prints? Make the place look so home-like, they do. No wonder you're so fond of it, Mole. Tell us all about it, and how you came to make it what it is."

Then, while the Rat busied himself fetching plates, and knives and forks, and mustard which he mixed in an egg-cup, the Mole, his bosom still heaving with the stress of his recent emotion, related— somewhat shyly at first, but with more freedom as he warmed to his subject—how this was planned, and how that was thought out, and how this was got through a windfall from an aunt, and that was a wonderful find and a bargain, and this other thing was bought out of laborious savings and a certain amount of "going without." His spirits finally quite restored, he must needs go and caress his possessions, and take a lamp and show off their points to his visitor and expatiate on them, quite forgetful of the supper they both so much needed; Rat, who was desperately hungry but strove to conceal it, nodding seriously, examining with a puckered brow, and saying, "wonderful," and "most remarkable," at intervals, when the chance for an observation was given him.

At last the Rat succeeded in decoying him to the table, and had just got seriously to work with the sardine-opener when sounds were heard from the fore-court without—sounds like the scuffling of small feet in the gravel and a confused murmur of tiny voices, while broken sentences reached them—"Now, all in a line—hold the lantern up a bit, Tommy—clear your throats first—no coughing after I say one, two, three.—Where's young Bill?—Here, come on, do, we're all a-waiting—"

"What's up?" inquired the Rat, pausing in his labours.

"I think it must be the field-mice," replied the Mole, with a touch of pride in his manner. "They go round carol-singing regularly at this time of the year. They're quite an institution in these parts. And they never pass me over—they come to Mole End last of all; and I used to give them hot drinks, and supper too sometimes, when I could afford it. It will be like old times to hear them again."

"Let's have a look at them!" cried the Rat, jumping up and running to the door.

It was a pretty sight, and a seasonable one, that met their eyes when they flung the door open. In the fore-court, lit by the dim rays of a horn lantern, some eight or ten little field-mice stood in a semicircle, red worsted comforters round their throats, their fore-paws thrust deep into their pockets, their feet jigging for warmth. With bright beady eyes they glanced shyly at each other, sniggering a little, sniffing and applying coat-sleeves a good deal. As the door opened, one of the elder ones that carried the lantern was just saying, "Now then, one, two, three!" and forthwith their shrill little voices uprose on the air, singing one of the old-time carols that their forefathers composed in fields that were fallow and held by frost, or when snow-bound in chimney corners, and handed down to be sung in the miry street to lamp-lit windows at Yule-time.

Carol

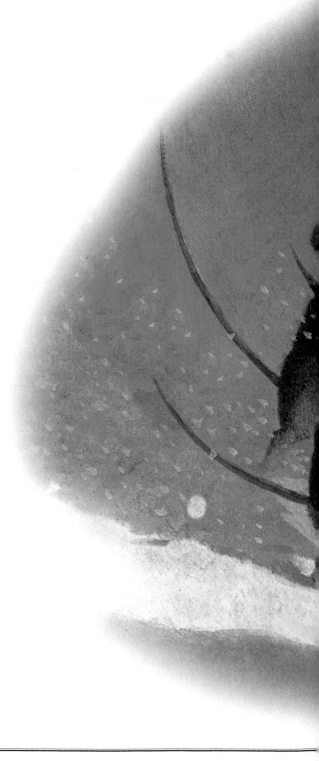

Villagers all, this frosty tide,
Let your doors swing open wide,
Though wind may follow, and snow beside,
Yet draw us in by your fire to bide;
      Joy shall be yours in the morning!

Here we stand in the cold and the sleet,
Blowing fingers and stamping feet,
Come from far away you to greet—
You by the fire and we in the street—
      Bidding you joy in the morning!

For ere one half of the night was gone,
Sudden a star has led us on,
Raining bliss and benison—
Bliss to-morrow and more anon,
      Joy for every morning!

Goodman Joseph toiled through the snow—
Saw the star o'er a stable low;
Mary she might not further go—
Welcome thatch, and litter below!
      Joy was hers in the morning!

And then they heard the angels tell
"Who were the first to cry Nowell?
Animals all, as it befell,
In the stable where they did dwell!
      Joy shall be theirs in the morning!"

The voices ceased, the singers, bashful but smiling, exchanged sidelong glances, and silence succeeded—but for a moment only. Then, from up above and far away, down the tunnel they had so lately travelled was borne to their ears in a faint musical hum the sound of distant bells ringing a joyful and clangorous peal.

"Very well sung, boys!" cried the Rat heartily. "And now come along in, all of you, and warm yourselves by the fire, and have something hot!"

"Yes, come along, field-mice," cried the Mole eagerly. "This is quite like old times! Shut the door after you. Pull up that settle to the fire. Now, you just wait a minute, while we—O, Ratty!" he cried in despair, plumping down on a seat, with tears impending. "Whatever are we doing? We've nothing to give them!"

"You leave all that to me," said the masterful Rat. "Here, you with the lantern! Come over this way. I want to talk to you. Now, tell me, are there any shops open at this hour of the night?"

"Why, certainly, sir," replied the field-mouse respectfully. "At this time of the year our shops keep open to all sorts of hours."

"Then look here!" said the Rat. "You go off at once, you and your lantern, and you get me—"

Here much muttered conversation ensued, and the Mole only heard bits of it, such as—"Fresh, mind!—no, a pound of that will do—see you get Buggins's, for I won't have any other—no, only the best—if you can't get it there, try somewhere else—yes, of course, homemade, no tinned stuff—well then, do the best you can!" Finally, there was a chink of coin passing from paw to paw, the field-mouse was provided with an ample basket for his purchases, and off he hurried, he and his lantern.

The rest of the field-mice, perched in a row on the settle, their small legs swinging, gave themselves up to enjoyment of the fire, and toasted their chilblains till they tingled; while the Mole, failing to

draw them into easy conversation, plunged into family history and made each of them recite the names of his numerous brothers, who were too young, it appeared, to be allowed to go out a-carolling this year, but looked forward very shortly to winning the parental consent.

The Rat, meanwhile, was busy examining the label on one of the beer-bottles. "I perceive this to be Old Burton," he remarked approvingly. "*Sensible* Mole! The very thing! Now we shall be able to mull some ale! Get the things ready, Mole, while I draw the corks."

It did not take long to prepare the brew and thrust the tin heater well into the red heart of the fire; and soon every field-mouse was sipping and coughing and choking (for a little mulled ale goes a long way) and wiping his eyes and laughing and forgetting he had ever been cold in his life.

"They act plays, too, these fellows," the Mole explained to the Rat. "Make them up all by themselves, and act them afterwards. And very well they do it, too! They gave us a capital one last year, about a field-mouse who was captured at sea by a Barbary corsair, and made to row in a galley; and when he escaped and got home again, his lady-love had gone into a convent. Here, *you*! You were in it, I remember. Get up and recite a bit."

The field-mouse addressed got up on his legs, giggled shyly, looked round the room, and remained absolutely tongue-tied. His comrades cheered him on, Mole coaxed and encouraged him, and the Rat went so far as to take him by the shoulders and shake him; but nothing could overcome his stage-fright. They were all busily engaged on him like watermen applying the Royal Humane Society's regulations to a case of long submersion, when the latch clicked, the door opened, and the field-mouse with the lantern reappeared, staggering under the weight of his basket.

There was no more talk of play-acting once the very real and solid contents of the basket had been tumbled out on the table. Under the generalship of Rat, everybody was set to do something or to fetch something. In a very few minutes supper was ready, and Mole, as he took the head of the table in a sort of dream, saw a lately barren board set thick with savoury comforts; saw his little friends' faces brighten and beam as they fell to without delay; and then let himself loose—for he was famished indeed—on the provender so magically provided, thinking what a happy home-coming this had turned out, after all. As they ate, they talked of old times, and the field-mice gave him the local gossip up to date, and answered as well as they could the hundred questions he had to ask them. The Rat said little or nothing, only taking care that each guest had what he wanted, and plenty of it, and that Mole had no trouble or anxiety about anything.

They clattered off at last, very grateful and showering wishes of the season, with their jacket pockets stuffed with remembrances for the small brothers and sisters at home. When the door had closed on the last of them and the chink of the lanterns had died away, Mole and Rat kicked the fire up, drew their chairs in, brewed themselves a last nightcap of mulled ale, and dis-cussed the events of the long day.

Jolly Old Saint Nicholas

TRADITIONAL CAROL

Jolly Old Saint Nicholas,
Lean your ear this way!
Don't you tell a single soul
What I'm going to say;
Christmas Eve is coming soon;
Now, you dear old man,
Whisper what you'll bring to me;
Tell me if you can.

When the clock is striking twelve,
When I'm fast asleep,
Down the chimney broad and black,
With your pack you'll creep;
All the stockings you will find
Hanging in a row;
Mine will be the shortest one,
You'll be sure to know.

Johnny wants a pair of skates;
Susy wants a dolly;
Nellie wants a story book;
She thinks dolls are folly;
As for me, my little brain
Isn't very bright;
Choose for me, old Santa Claus,
What you think is right.

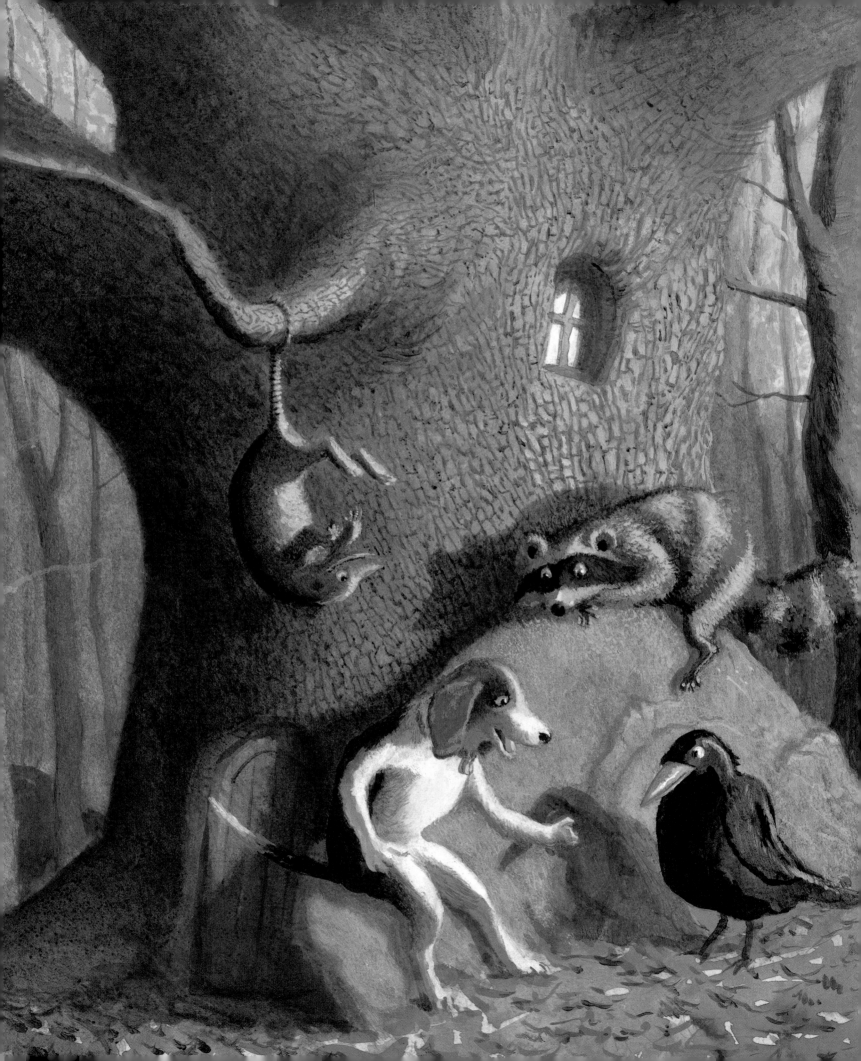

Christmas at the Hollow Tree Inn

ALBERT BIGELOW PAINE

ONCE UPON A TIME, when the Robin, and Turtle, and Squirrel, and Jack Rabbit had all gone home for the winter, nobody was left in the Hollow Tree except the 'Coon and 'Possum and the old black Crow. Of course the others used to come back and visit them pretty often, and Mr. Dog, too, now that he had got to be good friends with all the Deep Woods people, and they thought a great deal of him when they got to know him better. Mr. Dog told them a lot of things they had never heard of before, things that he'd learned at Mr. Man's house, and maybe that's one reason why they got to liking him so well.

He told them about Santa Claus, for one thing, and how the old fellow came down the chimney on Christmas Eve to bring presents to Mr. Man and his children, who always hung up their stockings for them, and Mr. Dog said that once he had hung up his stocking, too, and got a nice bone in it, that was so good he had buried and dug it up again as much as six times before spring. He said that Santa Claus always came to Mr. Man's house, and that whenever the children hung up their stockings they were always sure to get something in them.

Well, the Hollow Tree people had never heard of Santa Claus. They knew about Christmas, of course, because everybody, even the cows and sheep, knew about that; but they had never heard of Santa Claus. You see, Santa Claus only comes to Mr. Man's house, but they didn't know that either, so they thought if they just hung up their stockings he'd come there too, and that's what they made up their minds to do. They talked about it a great deal together, and Mr. 'Possum looked over all his stockings to pick out the biggest one he had, and Mr. Crow he made himself a new pair on purpose. Mr. 'Coon said he never knew Mr. Crow to make himself such big stockings before, but Mr. Crow said he was getting old and needed things bigger, and when he loaned one of his new stockings to Mr. 'Coon, Mr. 'Coon said, "That's so," and that he guessed they were about right, after all. They didn't tell anybody about it at first, but by and by they told Mr. Dog what they were going to do, and when Mr. Dog heard it he wanted to laugh right out. You see, he knew Santa Claus never went anywhere except to Mr. Man's house, and he thought it would be a great joke on the Hollow Tree people when they hung up their stockings and didn't get anything.

But by and by Mr. Dog thought about something else. He thought it would be too bad for them to be disappointed that way. You see, Mr. Dog liked them all now, and when he had thought about that a minute he made up his mind to do something. And this is what it was—he made up his mind to play Santa Claus!

He knew just how Santa Claus looked, 'cause he'd seen lots of pictures at Mr. Man's house, and he thought it would be great fun to dress up that way and take a bag of presents to the Hollow Tree while they were all asleep and fill up the stockings of the 'Coon and 'Possum and the old black Crow. But first he had to be sure of some way of getting in, so he said to them he didn't see how they could expect Santa Claus, their chimneys were so small, and Mr. Crow said they

could leave their latchstring out downstairs, which was just what
Mr. Dog wanted. Then they said they were going to have all the folks
that had spent summer with them over for Christmas dinner and to
see the presents they got in their stockings. They told Mr. Dog to
drop over too, if he could get away, and Mr. Dog said he would, and
went off laughing to himself and ran all the way home because he felt
so pleased at what he was going to do.

Well, he had to work pretty hard, I tell you, to get things ready.
It wasn't so hard to get the presents as it was to rig up his Santa Claus
dress. He found some long wool out in Mr. Man's barn for his white
whiskers, and he put some that wasn't so long on the edges of his
overcoat and boot tops and around an old hat he had. Then he
borrowed a big sack he found out there and fixed it up to swing over
his back, just as he had seen Santa Claus do in the pictures. He had
a lot of nice things to take along. Three tender young chickens he'd
borrowed from Mr. Man, for one thing, and then he bought some new
neckties for the Hollow Tree folks all around, and a big, striped candy
cane for each one, because candy canes always looked well sticking
out of a stocking. You see, Mr. Dog lived with Mr. Man, and didn't ever
have to buy much for himself, so he had always saved his money.
He had even more things than that, but I can't remember just now
what they were; and when he started out, all dressed up like Santa
Claus, I tell you his bag was pretty heavy, and he almost wished
before he got there that he hadn't started with quite so much.

It got heavier and heavier all the way, and he was glad enough to
get there and find the latchstring out. He set his bag down to rest a
minute before climbing the stairs, and then opened the doors softly
and listened. He didn't hear a thing except Mr. Crow and Mr. 'Coon
and Mr. 'Possum breathing pretty low, and he knew they might wake
up any minute, and he wouldn't have been caught there in the midst
of things for a good deal. So he slipped up just as easy as anything,

and when he got up in the big parlor room he almost had to laugh right out loud, for there were the stockings sure enough, all hung up in a row, and a card with a name on it over each one telling whom it belonged to.

Then he listened again, and all at once he jumped and held his breath, for he heard Mr. 'Possum say something. But Mr. 'Possum was only talking in his sleep, and saying "I'll take another piece, please," and Mr. Dog knew he was dreaming about the mince pie he'd had for supper.

So, then he opened his bag and filled the stockings. He put in mixed candy and nuts and little things first, and then the candy canes, so they'd show at the top, and hung a nice dressed chicken outside. I tell you, they looked fine! It almost made Mr. Dog wish he had a stocking of his own there to fill, and he forgot all about them waking up, and sat down in a chair to look at the stockings. It was a nice rocking chair, and over in a dark corner where they wouldn't be apt to see him, even if one of them did wake up and stick his head out of his room, so Mr. Dog felt pretty safe now anyway. He rocked softly, and looked and looked at the nice stockings, and thought how pleased they'd be in the morning, and how tired he was. You've heard about people being as tired as a dog; and that's just how Mr. Dog felt. He was so tired he didn't feel a bit like starting home, and by and by—he never did know how it happened—but by and by Mr. Dog went sound asleep right there in his chair, with all his Santa Claus clothes on.

And there he sat, with his empty bag in his hand and the nice full stockings in front of him, all night long. Even when it came morning and began to get light Mr. Dog didn't know it; he just slept right on, he was that tired. Then pretty soon the door of Mr. 'Possum's room opened and he poked out his head. And just then the door of Mr. 'Coon's room opened and he poked out his head. Then the door of the old black Crow opened and out poked his head. They all looked toward the stockings, and they didn't see Mr. Dog, or even each other, at all. They saw their stockings, though, and Mr. 'Coon said all at once:

"Oh, there's something in my stocking!"

And then Mr. Crow says: "Oh, there's something in my stocking, too!"

And Mr. 'Possum says: "Oh, there's something in all our stockings!"

And with that they gave a great hurrah all together, and rushed out and grabbed their stockings and turned around just in time to see Mr. Dog jump right straight up out of his chair, for he did not know where he was the least bit in the world.

"Oh, there's Santa Claus himself!" they all shouted together, and made a rush for their rooms, for they were scared almost to death. But it dawned on Mr. Dog in a second, and he commenced to laugh and hurrah to think what a joke it was on everybody. And when they heard Mr. Dog laugh they knew him right away, and they all came up and looked at him, and he had to tell just what he'd done and everything; so they emptied out their stockings on the floor and ate some of the presents and looked at the others, until they almost forgot about breakfast, just as children do on Christmas morning.

Then Mr. Crow said, all at once, that he'd make a little coffee, and that Mr. Dog must stay and have some, and by and by they made him promise to spend the day with them and be there when the Robin and the Squirrel and Mr. Turtle and Jack Rabbit came, which he did.

And it was snowing hard outside, which made it a nicer Christmas than if it hadn't been, and when all the others came they brought presents too. And when they saw Mr. Dog dressed up as Santa Claus and heard how he'd gone to sleep and been caught, they laughed and laughed. And it snowed so hard that they had to stay all night, and after dinner they sat around the fire and told stories. And they had to stay the next night too, and all that Christmas week. And I wish I could tell you all that happened that week, but I can't, because I haven't time. But it was the very nicest Christmas that ever was in the Hollow Tree, or in the Big Deep Woods anywhere.

The Friendly Beasts

TRADITIONAL CAROL

Jesus our brother, kind and good
 Was humbly born in a stable rude,
And the friendly beasts around him stood,
 Jesus our brother, kind and good.

"I," said the donkey, shaggy and brown,
 "I carried His mother up hill and down;
I carried her safely to Bethlehem town."
 "I," said the donkey, shaggy and brown.

"I," said the cow all white and red,
 "I gave Him my manger for His bed;
I gave Him my hay to pillow His head."
 "I," said the cow all white and red.

"I," said the sheep with curly horn,
 "I gave Him my wool for His blanket warm;
He wore my coat on Christmas morn."
 "I," said the sheep with curly horn.

"I," said the dove from the rafters high,
 "I cooed Him to sleep so He would not cry;
We cooed Him to sleep, my mate and I."
 "I," said the dove from the rafters high.

Thus every beast by some good spell,
 In the stable dark was glad to tell
Of the gift he gave Immanuel,
 The gift he gave Immanuel.

A Visit from St. Nicholas

CLEMENT CLARKE MOORE

'TWAS THE NIGHT before Christmas, when all through the house
Not a creature was stirring, not even a mouse.
The stockings were hung by the chimney with care,
In hopes that St. Nicholas soon would be there.
The children were nestled all snug in their beds,
While visions of sugar plums danced in their heads;
And mamma in her kerchief, and I in my cap,
Had just settled our brains for a long winter's nap—

When out on the lawn there arose such a clatter,
I sprang from my bed to see what was the matter.
Away to the window I flew like a flash,
Tore open the shutters and threw up the sash.
The moon, on the breast of the new-fallen snow,
Gave a luster of midday to objects below;
When what to my wondering eyes should appear,
But a miniature sleigh and eight tiny reindeer,
With a little old driver, so lively and quick
I knew in a moment it must be St. Nick.

More rapid than eagles his coursers they came,
And he whistled and shouted and called them by name:
"Now, Dasher! now, Dancer! now, Prancer and Vixen!
On, Comet! on, Cupid! on, Donder and Blitzen!
To the top of the porch, to the top of the wall!
Now dash away, dash away, dash away all!"
As dry leaves that before the wild hurricane fly,
When they meet with an obstacle, mount to the sky,
So, up to the housetop the coursers they flew,
With a sleigh full of toys—and St. Nicholas too.

And then in a twinkling I heard on the roof
The prancing and pawing of each little hoof.
As I drew in my head and was turning around,
Down the chimney St. Nicholas came with a bound.
He was dressed all in fur from his head to his foot,
And his clothes were all tarnished with ashes and soot;
A bundle of toys he had flung on his back,
And he looked like a peddler just opening his pack.

His eyes, how they twinkled! his dimples, how merry!
His cheeks were like roses, his nose like a cherry;
His droll little mouth was drawn up like a bow,
And the beard on his chin was as white as the snow.
The stump of a pipe he held tight in his teeth,
And the smoke, it encircled his head like a wreath.
He had a broad face, and a little round belly
That shook, when he laughed, like a bowl full of jelly.
He was chubby and plump—a right jolly old elf—
And I laughed when I saw him, in spite of myself.

A wink of his eye and a twist of his head
Soon gave me to know I had nothing to dread.
He spoke not a word, but went straight to his work,
And filled all the stockings; then turned with a jerk,
And laying his finger aside of his nose,
And giving a nod, up the chimney he rose.
He sprang to his sleigh, to his team gave a whistle,
And away they all flew like the down of a thistle;

But I heard him exclaim, ere he drove out of sight:
"Happy Christmas to all, and to all a good night!"